John Thomps
MELODY ALL THE WAY!

PIANO TUITION ON A TUNEFUL BASIS

GRADE I-plus

WILLIS MUSIC COMPANY
Cincinnati

© 1949 & 1963 The Willis Music Co.

Exclusive distributors:
Music Sales Limited, 8/9 Frith Street, London W1V 5TZ.
Music Sales Pty Limited, 120 Rothschild Avenue, Rosebery, NSW 2018, Australia

Reproducing this music in any form is illegal and forbidden
by the Copyright, Designs and Patents Act 1988.

FOREWORD

The MELODY ALL THE WAY series is published in response to the insistent plea of countless piano teachers who fully subscribe to the author's standards of teaching material and teaching ideas, but who find themselves in a quandary when two children are studying in the same family, or where neighbouring children "start" together. The heartaches that naturally arise if one child progresses somewhat faster than the other are obviated if the youngsters are not using identical books.

The MELODY ALL THE WAY series is planned not to *supplant* the MODERN COURSE FOR THE PIANO, but as *interchangeable* with that work. Some teachers find it sound practice to use two study books simultaneously—one, of course, serving the purpose of a supplementary book for sight-reading and additional practice material Grade 1 of MELODY ALL THE WAY would be ideal for this use in connection with the *first half* of " The First Grade Book "from THE MODERN COURSE FOR THE PIANO.

It should be observed that each Course is complete in itself, permitting individual or interchangeable use.

FAMILIAR AIRS

In so far as possible, the musical examples in MELODY ALL THE WAY have been adapted from familiar airs—folk tunes, themes from symphonies, well-known piano solos, songs, etc. This has an advantage for the young student: getting away from cut-and-dried text, and giving him the thrill of performing, in simplified versions, music which is frequently heard on the radio, gramophone records, etc.

PLAYING WITH EXPRESSION

There is no sound reason why the elementary pianist should not be required to play with *musical expression* and *understanding*. The simplest melody can be interesting if played with definite intention. Real interpretation consists of more than simply following the marks of dynamics. It includes *colour*—the result of employing various Touches.

Even a beginner can master the Touches. Taught in their fundamental form, they offer no real problem, and the result in stimulating real musicianship will richly reward the efforts of teacher and pupil alike.

HANON: PRELIMINARY EXERCISES –FOR DEVELOPING THE TOUCHES

John Thompson's edition of the Hanon Preliminary Exercises is carefully designed to develop the fundamental touches. The studies are arranged in Crotchets, and each page is attractively illustrated and titled.

The Phrasing Touch, Finger Legato, Finger Staccato, Wrist Staccato, Forearm Staccato and Legato, Portamento, Rotary Motion, etc., are treated in consecutive order.

To accomplish *maximum* results, these Hanon Exercises should be started early in Book 1 and continued throughout the progress of Book 2. The improvement in interpretation will become readily apparent.

TEMPO

While each example bears a Tempo indication—*Moderato, Andante, Allegro*, etc., the *actual* rate of speed should be decided by the teacher, since pupils vary so widely in ability. While encouraging an increased tempo in review work, the wise teacher never allows speed to go beyond the point of *precision*—always a most important objective.

CERTIFICATE OF MERIT

A Certificate of Merit has been included on page 43 as recognition of successful completion of this book. It should be signed and dated by the teacher.

J. T.

W.M.Co.6603
(46347)

CONTENTS

FOREWORD...... 3

THUMB UNDER
"Waltz"......*Joh. Strauss* 6

THUMB UNDER
Theme from the Opera, "Zampa"......*Hérold* 7

NEW KEY—D Major
"The Mill"......*Jensen* 8

THUMB UNDER
"Melody in F"......*Rubinstein* 9

NEW KEY—A Major
"Waltz"......*Schubert* 10

CHORD PLAYING
"Funeral March"......*Chopin* 11

TWO-NOTE PHRASES IN LEAPS
"Humoresque"......*Dvořák* 12

STRETCH—Thumb to Fifth Finger
"Rondino"......*Beethoven* 14

TWO-PART PLAYING
Polonaise......*Bach* 15

DOTTED QUAVERS
Toreador March from "Carmen"......*Bizet* 16

CHORDS IN DOTTED QUAVERS
Bridal Procession from "Lohengrin"......*Wagner* 17

NEW KEY—E Flat Major
"Wings"...... 18

LEFT HAND MELODY PLAYING
Theme from "Unfinished Symphony"......*Schubert* 19

RECITAL PIECE
"Just a Song at Twilight"......*Molloy* 20

NEW KEY—E Major
Theme from "Rondo Capriccioso"......*Mendelssohn* 22

CONTRASTING LEGATO AND STACCATO
La Donna è Mobile from "Rigoletto"......*Verdi* 23

NEW KEY—A Flat Major
"Day Dreams"...... 24

SOSTENUTO MARK
Theme from "Rhapsody No. 12"......*Liszt* 26

D.S. AL FINE
Theme from "Rosamunde"......*Schubert* 27

Theme from "Nocturne"......*Chopin* 28

Theme from "Rhapsody No. 2"......*Liszt* 30

Theme from "March Militaire"......*Schubert* 32

CHORD PLAYING
"Prelude in C Minor"......*Chopin* 34

SEMIQUAVERS
"Under the Leaves"......*Thomé* 35

Theme from "Gipsy Rondo"......*Haydn* 36

Theme from "Valse", Op. 34, No. 2......*Chopin* 37

Themes from "Washington Post March"......*Sousa* 38

CHRISTMAS CAROLS

"Jolly Old Saint Nicholas"...... 40

"God Rest You Merry, Gentlemen"...... 41

GLOSSARY OF TERMS, SIGNS AND ABBREVIATIONS...... 42

CERTIFICATE OF MERIT...... 43

THUMB UNDER

Sept. 28

left hand only

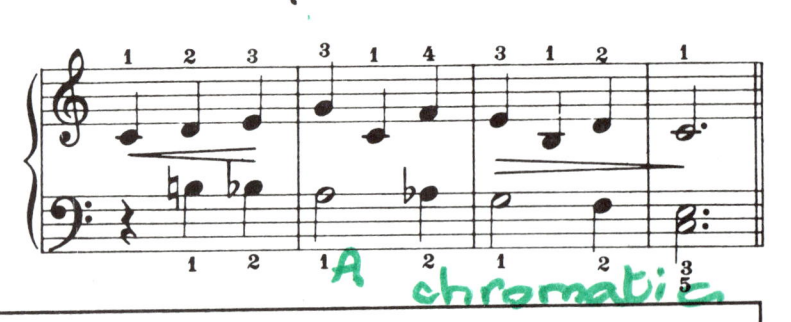

From
WALTZ

Allegretto

Johann Strauss

chromatic

Teacher's Note

At this point the pupil should be assigned John Thompson's FIRST GRADE STUDIES. A description of the book appears below.

John THOMPSON *First Grade* **STUDIES** *Twenty four studies for the development of fingers, wrist and forearm: employing five-finger groups, broken chords and examples in phrasing.*

Chappell & Co Ltd
50, New Bond Street London W.1
The Willis Music Company
Cincinnati Ohio

This book is intended to lay a foundation in technique for the FIRST GRADE piano student. The author has kept in mind the fact that all examples, even technical exercises, must be tuneful if the young pupil's interest is to be retained.

Only elementary pianistic figures have been employed, built for the most part on five-finger groups (the forerunner of the scale) and broken triads (preparation for extended arpeggios to follow later on). Properly used, the book becomes at once a means of developing *Independence, Strength* and *Evenness of Finger Action*, together with *Reading and Expression.*

Examples in *Phrasing, Wrist Staccato* and the use of the *Forearm* have been included.

Copyright, MCMXLIX, © MCMLXIII, by The Willis Music Co.
Chappell & Co. Ltd., 50 *New Bond Street, London, W.1*
International Copyright Secured

W.M.Co.6603
(46347)

Made in England

THUMB UNDER
Preparatory Studies

Zampa was a pirate in the Opera of that name.

Camille, the heroine of the opera, is alarmed for her father's safety as he sets out to meet his incoming fleet of ships, threatened by the pirates.

She sings the air shown here as she prays for his safe return.

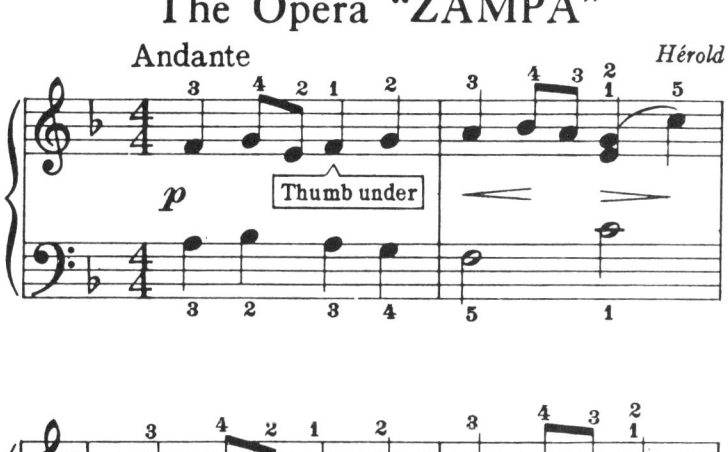

From
The Opera "ZAMPA"

Andante — Hérold

NEW KEY — D MAJOR

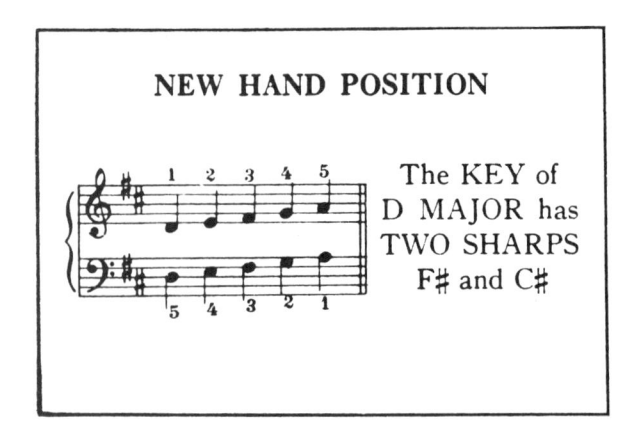

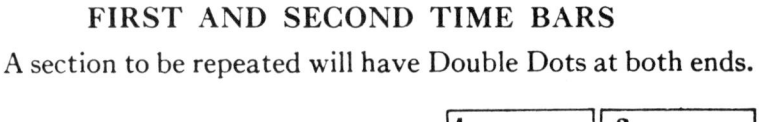

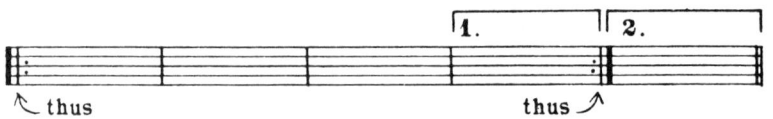

NEW HAND POSITION

The KEY of D MAJOR has TWO SHARPS F♯ and C♯

FIRST AND SECOND TIME BARS

A section to be repeated will have Double Dots at both ends.

↶ thus   thus ↗

After playing through the SECOND time do NOT play the FIRST TIME BAR; instead, go direct to the SECOND.

From
THE MILL
Adolf Jensen

Allegro moderato

Play the Scale and Broken Chord of D Major.

ANTON RUBINSTEIN was born in Russia and when he was five showed great talent. At the age of eleven the great Liszt proclaimed him a genius.

One of the most popular compositions he ever wrote was the "Melody in F", which is still a favourite with piano students.

From
MELODY in F

Moderato

Anton Rubinstein

NEW KEY—A MAJOR

Hand Position

The KEY of A MAJOR has THREE SHARPS—
F♯, C♯ and G♯

Practise the Left Hand alone first as a Preparatory Study.

Oh, gentle Franz Schubert we all salute you,
Beautiful Music we sing to-day.
Comes echo'ing clear from happier ages
When Old Vienna was young and gay.

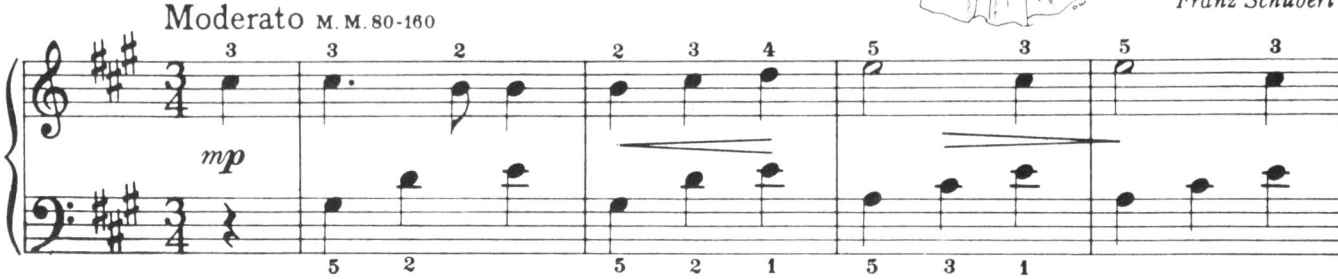

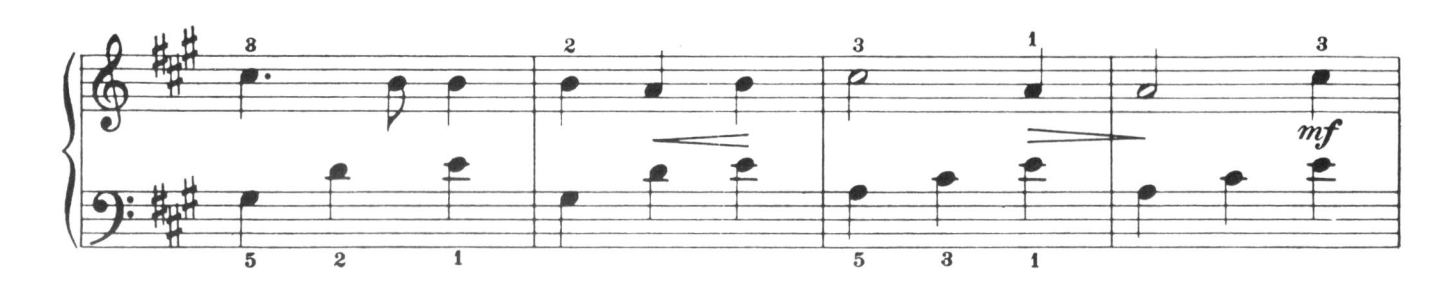

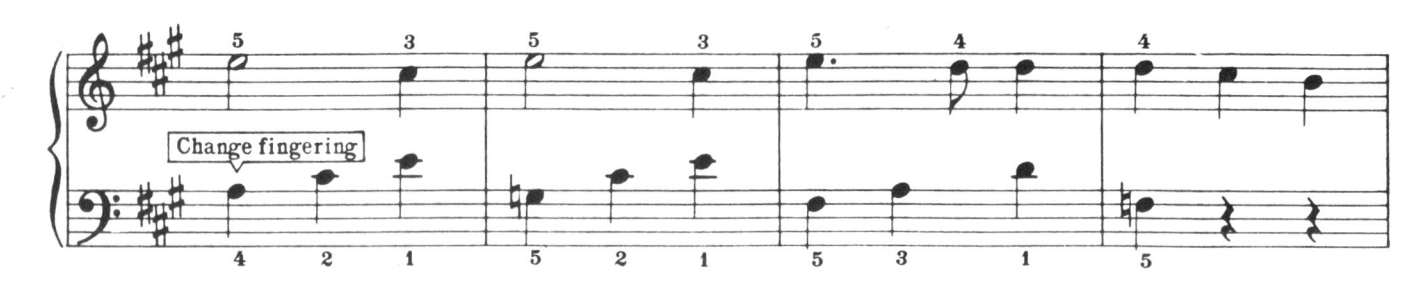

From WALTZ

Franz Schubert

Moderato M.M. 80-160

Change fingering

Play the Scale and Broken Chord of A Major

W.M.Co.6603

From
FUNERAL MARCH

Very slowly and solemnly

Frédéric Chopin

Suggestion for supplementary solo in sheet form.

PROCESSION OF THE SEVEN DWARFS by Lois Long is a fine follow-up piece with both hands in the Bass Clef.

W. M. Co. 6603

TWO NOTE PHRASES IN LEAPS

Themes

From

HUMORESQUE

Anton Dvořák

13

LUDWIG VAN BEETHOVEN was born in Bonn, a city on the River Rhine. He began to study music when he was four years old, and at eight he also played the violin very well. Beethoven is acknowledged as the greatest instrumental composer the world has produced. He had a very busy and full life; much joy and many sorrows. His magnificent music is played by all the great orchestras to this day. Listen when next a Beethoven Symphony is programmed on the radio. The musical world is eternally indebted to the composer for the wealth of his creative thought.

LUDWIG VAN BEETHOVEN
1770 - 1827

From
RONDINO
Ludwig van Beethoven

D. S. al Fine

D. S. (Dal Segno) al fine means go back to sign (𝄋) and play to *Fine*

W. M. Co. 6603

POLONAISE—While classed as a dance rhythm, the *Polonaise* is in reality more of a procession than a dance.

It was used in court ceremonies where the nobility marched to its stately measures past the throne in homage to royalty.

It should always be played in "big" and majestic style and in march tempo.

Polonaise

J. S. Bach

THE DOTTED QUAVER

MARCH OF THE TOREADORS

From
The Opera "CARMEN"

Georges Bizet

In March Tempo

NEW KEY—B♭ MAJOR

B Flat Major has
TWO FLATS
B♭ and E♭

BRIDAL CHORUS
From The Opera "LOHENGRIN"

Slow March Time

Richard Wagner

NEW KEY—E♭ MAJOR

E Flat Major has
THREE FLATS
B♭, E♭ and A♭

WINGS

Up above the houses glides the soaring plane
Cutting through the clouds and back to sun again;
You can be the captain of a ship at sea,
Just to fly a plane would be the life for me!

MELODY IN THE LEFT HAND
Right Hand Staccato Thirds

FRANZ SCHUBERT is known as the greatest song writer that ever lived. He was born in Austria near Vienna and when he was ten years old he was singing in a church choir, and had already composed some little songs and piano pieces.

The music of Schubert comes into our homes constantly over the radio. This master lived only 31 years and yet he wrote more than 1,100 compositions; and of these nearly 600 are songs.

From
THE UNFINISHED SYMPHONY

Andante moderato

Franz Schubert

Oct. 7th.

Try to find out the other words from your grandparents

From
JUST A SONG AT TWILIGHT

J. L. Molloy

Andante

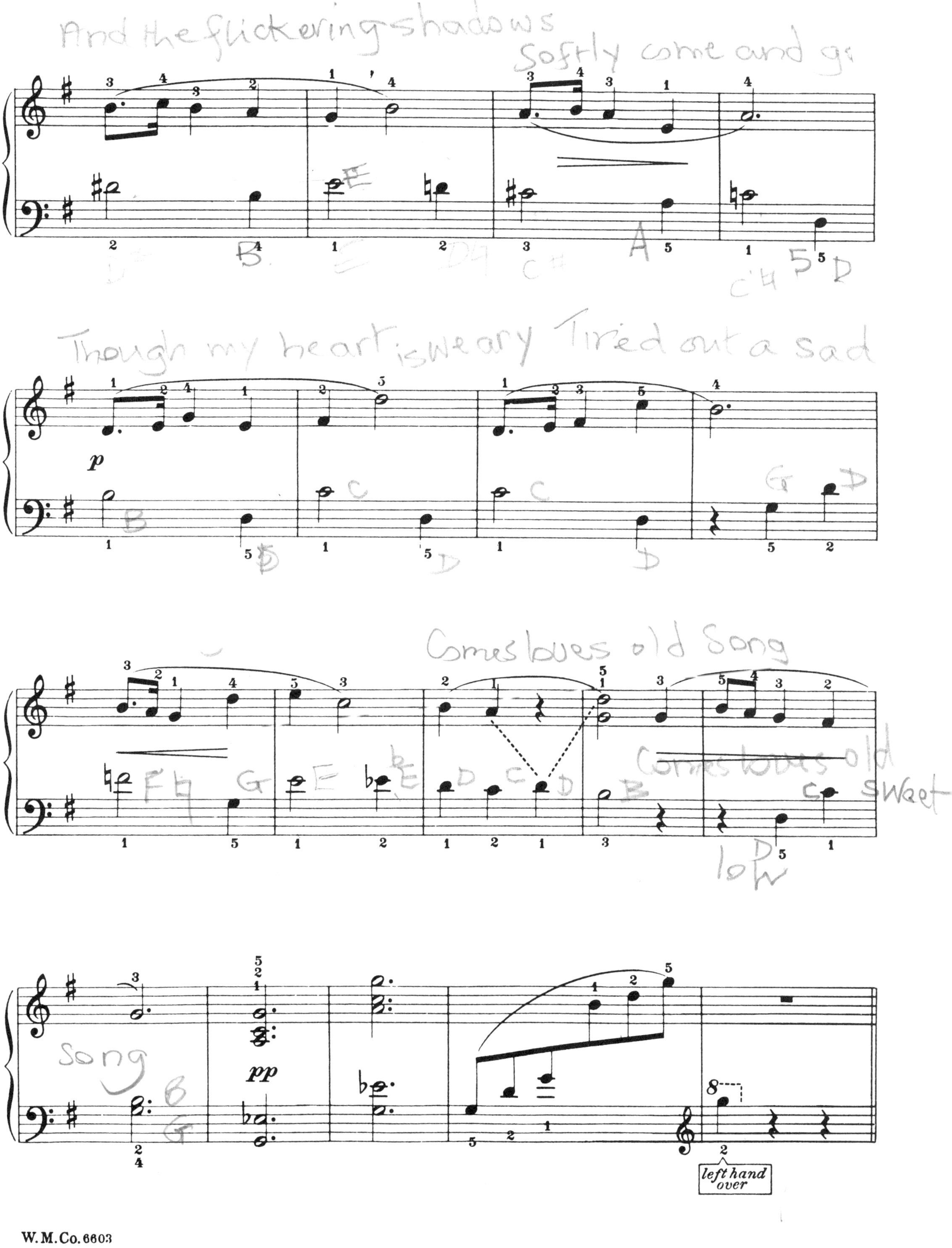
left hand over

NEW KEY—E MAJOR

1st Position   **2nd Position**

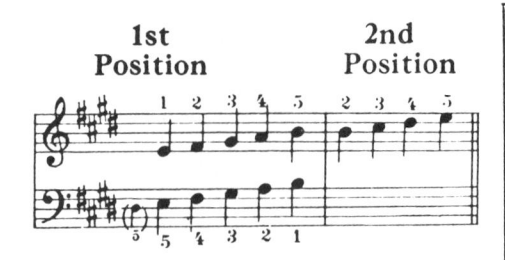

The KEY of E MAJOR has FOUR SHARPS—F#, C#, G# and D#.

FELIX MENDELSSOHN was born in Hamburg, Germany of wealthy and musical parents.

At eleven years of age he was already seriously interested in composition. He loved fairy stories and much of his music reflects this liking.

He wrote many beautiful piano pieces and the "Rondo Capriccioso" is one of the most famous.

From "RONDO CAPRICCIOSO"

Felix Mendelssohn

Allegro molto

GIUSEPPE VERDI was born to a poor inn-keeper and his wife who lived at the foot of the Apennine Mountains.

In his time Italy was ruled by a foreign nation and as Verdi's operas all breathed patriotism, he was the idol of his country.

The little composition which you are now to study, is one of the most popular and lasting airs ever written. You will have heard it many times on your radio.

LA DONNA È MOBILE
from the Opera "RIGOLETTO"

Giuseppe Verdi

NEW KEY—A♭ MAJOR

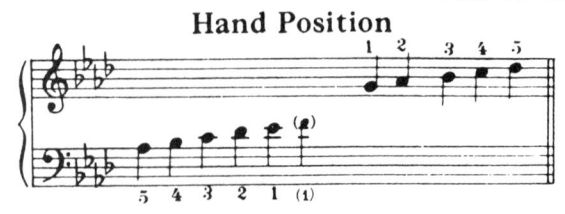

Hand Position

The KEY of A♭ MAJOR has FOUR FLATS—
B♭, E♭, A♭ and D♭

Play the following piece with your best singing tone.

Lily, lily, white and gold,
Gleaming from the water cold,
You shall reign like any queen
'Til the Autumn winds grow keen.

DAY DREAMS

Andante moderato

25

Preparatory Exercise

HUNGARIAN RHAPSODIE
No. 12

From

Franz Liszt

Andantino

From
"ROSAMUNDE"

Allegro animato

Franz Schubert

Singing Touch

At this stage the first book of TUNEFUL TECHNIC might be usefully employed. These melodious finger-drills consist of familiar melodies alternating between the hands, which integrate with the figure-patterns of well-known studies.

FREDERIC CHOPIN
1810-1849

When Frédéric Chopin was a little boy, the Polish people called him a second Mozart, and we know that he played a concerto in public before he was nine years old. He was very imaginative and sensitive to beauty, and one great Polish actor expressed the opinion that he would have done well on the stage. He wrote a great deal of beautiful music during his short life-time, including nineteen Nocturnes.

The word Nocturne means night song. The following is an adaptation of one of his best-loved 'night songs'.

From
NOCTURNE
Frédéric Chopin

29

FRANZ LISZT was born in a little town in Hungary. He was a child-wonder—playing a public concert at the age of nine. Many of his compositions are inspired by Hungarian Gipsy themes.

He was a most brilliant pianist and a beloved teacher, helping and inspiring many pupils who became concert artists.

Born 1811 — Died 1886

Liszt at the age of 14
Courtesy "The Musical Quarterly"

From
HUNGARIAN RHAPSODIE
No. 2

Allegro molto

Franz Liszt

31

From
MARCHE MILITAIRE

Franz Schubert

In brisk March Tempo

Watch the fingering as the hands change position.

CHORD PLAYING

Among the many beautiful and immortal works of Chopin are the Twenty-Four Preludes—one in each major and minor key.

The Prelude on this page is an adaptation of one of the most popular of these beloved piano compositions.

At Prince Radziwill's in 1829

From
PRELUDE IN C MINOR

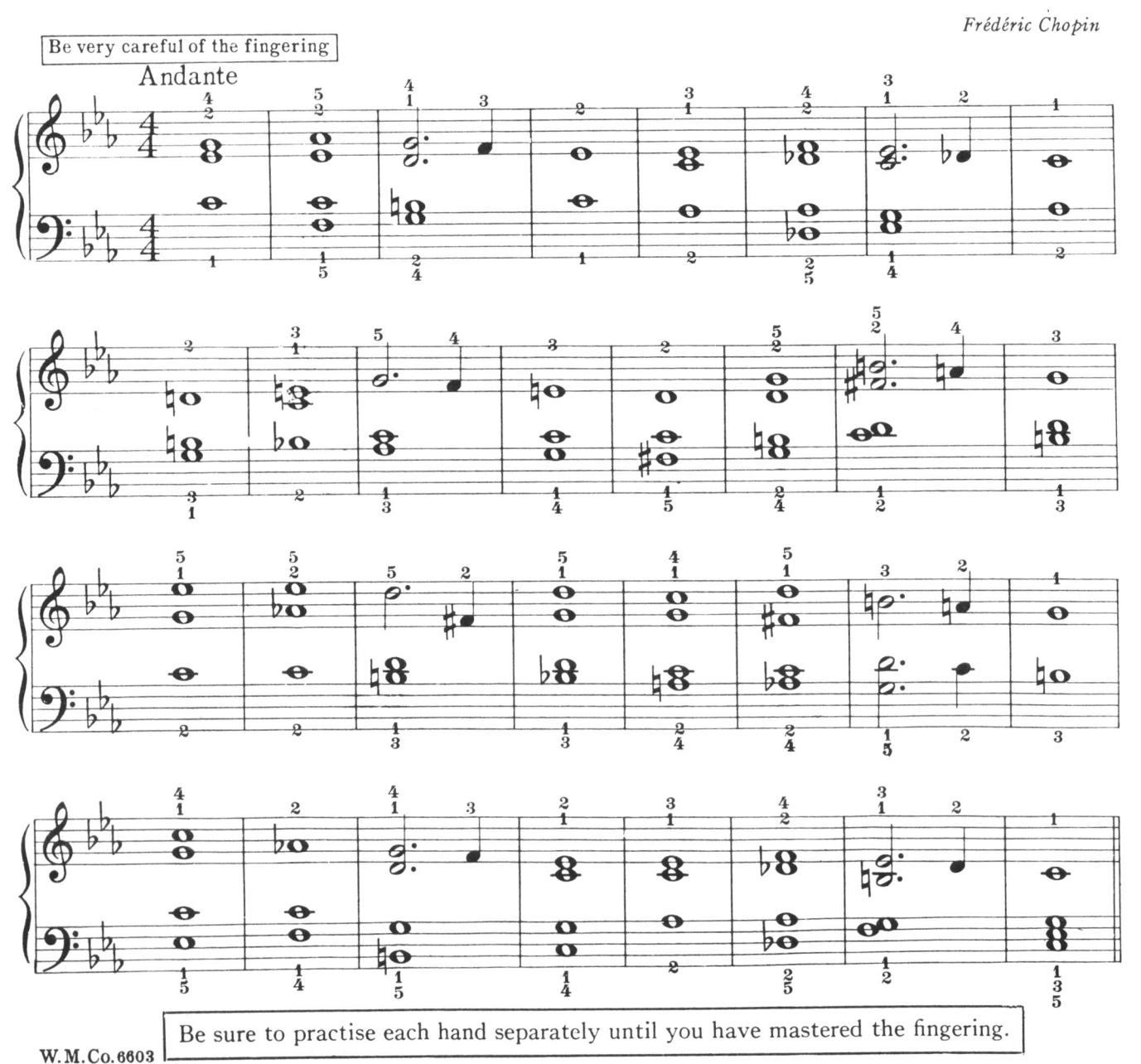

Frédéric Chopin

Be very careful of the fingering

Andante

Be sure to practise each hand separately until you have mastered the fingering.

SEMIQUAVERS
From
UNDER THE LEAVES

Thomé

From
GYPSY RONDO
Franz Josef Haydn

8va - - - - - - = play an octave higher than written.

PREPARATORY STUDIES

From
VALSE, Op. 34, No 2

Frédéric Chopin

JOHN PHILIP SOUSA was born in Washington, D. C. He became an eminent band-master and probably the most popular composer of band marches the world has produced. He was known as "The March King". When he was eight years old he was playing violin in a dancing school and at the age of sixteen, conducted a theatre orchestra. His best known marches are "The Stars and Stripes Forever", "High School Cadets" and "The Washington Post March".

From
THE WASHINGTON POST MARCH

John Philip Sousa

39

JOLLY OLD SAINT NICHOLAS

Traditional

Allegretto

Jol-ly old Saint Nich-o-las, Lean your ear this way! Don't you tell a sin-gle soul What I'm going to say; Christ-mas Eve is com-ing soon, Now you dear old man, Whis-per what you'll bring to me; Tell me if you can.

2. When the clock is striking twelve,
    When I'm fast asleep,
Down the chimney broad and black,
    With your pack you'll creep;
All the stockings you will find
    Hanging in a row;
Mine will be the shortest one,
    You'll be sure to know.

3. Johnny wants a pair of skates;
    Susy wants a sled;
Nellie wants a picture book;
    Yellow, blue and red;
Now I think I'll leave to you
    What to give the rest;
Choose for me, dear Santa Claus,
    You will know the best.

GOD REST YOU MERRY, GENTLEMEN

Old English

Moderato

God rest you mer-ry, gen-tle-men, Let noth-ing you dis-may, Re-mem-ber Christ our Sav-iour Was born on Christ-mas day, To save us all from Sa-tan's pow'r, When we were gone a-stray. O ti-dings of com-fort and joy, com-fort and joy, O ti-dings of com-fort and joy.

2. From God, our heav'nly Father,
   A blessed angel came;
   And unto certain shepherds
   Brought tidings of the same;
   How that in Bethlehem was born
   The Son of God by name.
   Refrain.

3. The shepherds at those tidings,
   Rejoiced much in mind,
   And left their flocks a-feeding,
   In tempest, storm, and wind;
   And went to Bethlehem straightway,
   The Son of God to find.
   Refrain.

GLOSSARY OF TERMS, SIGNS AND ABBREVIATIONS USED IN THIS BOOK

Signs or Abbreviations	Terms	Meaning
>	accent	To emphasize or stress a certain note or beat
	allegretto	Light and lively
	allegro	Fast
	andante	Slow
	andantino	Slow—but not as slow as *andante*
	animato	With animation
	arpeggio	In the style of a harp—broken chord
	a tempo	Resume original tempo
⟨	crescendo	A gradual increase in the tone
D.C.	Da Capo	Return to beginning
D.C. al Fine	Da Capo al Fine	Return to beginning and play to *Fine*
⟩	diminuendo	A gradual decrease in the tone
	espressivo	Expressively
Fine	Finale	The end
f	forte	Loud
ff	fortissimo	Very loud
	largo	Very slowly
	legato	Connected, bound together
mf	mezzo forte	Moderately loud
mp	mezzo piano	Moderately soft
	moderato	At a moderate tempo
	molto	Much
	Nocturne	Night Song
8va or 8	octave above	Play all notes under this sign one octave higher than written
⌒	pause	To hold or pause, according to taste
p	piano	Softly
pp	pianissimo	Very softly
	poco	Little
rit.	ritard	A gradual slowing of the tempo
	sostenuto	Sustained—with singing quality
	staccato	Detached
	tempo	Time—rate of speed

Certificate of Merit

This certifies that

....

has successfully completed

GRADE 1 - PLUS

OF

JOHN THOMPSON'S
"MELODY ALL THE WAY"

and is eligible for promotion to

GRADE 2

....
Teacher

Date ....

Seal — John Thompson's Melody All The Way